Introduction to Street Law in India

Siva Prasad Bose

Published by Joy Bose, 2022.

Street Law in India

By Siva Prasad Bose and Joy Bose

Published by Joy Bose

Contents

Dedication

This book is dedicated to the constitution of India, which is the source from which all laws in India derive.

Preface

Law touches every aspect of our daily lives, yet many in India remain unaware of the laws that govern and protect them. From workplace rights to consumer protection, from inheritance disputes to online fraud, understanding the law is essential for navigating modern society.

This book is designed to be a practical guide to the everyday legal challenges that people face. Whether it's dealing with unfair dismissal from a job, filing an FIR, understanding traffic rules, or protecting yourself from cybercrime, this book aims to demystify the legal landscape and provide you with the knowledge you need to make informed decisions.

In the USA, there is a book and initiative called "Street Law" that is used to teach youngsters about relevant laws that may apply to them. This book is in a way inspired by that and brings a similar approach to India. Our goal is to bridge the gap between complex legal language and real-world scenarios, offering clear, actionable insights into how the law works in various situations. By equipping yourself with legal knowledge, you not only protect your rights but also contribute to a society where fairness and justice prevail. We hope this book serves as a useful companion in your journey to legal empowerment.

Chapter 1: What is Street Law?

Street law is everyday law. It is the law that is applicable to people 'on the street'. Millions of us are affected by the law on a daily basis but are unaware of the applicable Indian laws and hence cannot take advantage of it when we need its protection. For example, if we are dismissed from our job arbitrarily and unfairly, we may not be aware that there are labor laws applicable on basis of which we can be protected from unfair dismissal. That is why it is important for all of us to be aware of how the law affects us.

1.1 What is law?

The question "what is law" has troubled people for many years. An entire active field of study known as "jurisprudence" (the study of law and legal philosophy) is devoted to answering this question. Many definitions of law exist. Laws can be defined as the rules and regulations made and enforced by the government that regulate the conduct of people within a society. Rules made and enforced by the government are called laws. The government makes laws that affect almost every aspect of daily life.

Every society that has ever existed has recognized the need for laws. These laws may have been unwritten, but even the pre-industrial societies, such as ancient and medieval India, had rules to regulate people's conduct. Without laws, there would be confusion and disorder. A democratic system of government cannot function effectively unless its laws are respected. In other words, society must be based on the "rule of law". This means that all members of society must follow the law and it should be applicable equally to all.

1.2 Law and values

Laws generally reflect and promote a society's values. Our legal system is influenced by our society's traditional ideas of right and wrong. Laws against murder, for example, reflect the moral belief that killing another person is wrong.

Street law is law that has been of practical use in everyday life. Daily activities such as making a purchase (contract law) marriage and divorce (marriage law such as Hindu Marriage Act or Special Marriage Act), crime (criminal law) or traffic violation places citizens face to face with the law. Street law is designed to provide one the understanding of legal issues and the ability to analyze, evaluate and in same situation resolve legal disputes.

Street law addresses general problems in the areas of criminal justice, torts, consumer laws, family law and so on. It helps us to learn what to do if we become a victim of crime, when and how to select an attorney, the legal rights and responsibilities of parents and children, how to advocate for change in our community, how to solve problems without going to court and what to do about discrimination and other violations of our constitutional rights. It is designed to help us become better and more active citizens committed to basic human rights and freedoms.

1.3 Law Making in the Supreme Court of India

The law declared by the supreme court shall be binding on all courts within the territory of India [Article 141 of the Indian constitution].

Binding force of supreme court decisions: All courts in India are bound to follow the decisions of the supreme court [AIR 1955 Nagpur 293].

The law laid down by the Supreme court of India is binding on all lower courts and tribunals [AIR 1995 SC 1349]. Where the supreme court has stated that the law laid down in a particular case is the applicable law, the high court cannot consider or rely on any supposedly conflicting decision. If the Supreme Court contradicts the law declared in another case, the previous law stands overruled. [1998 8 SCC 275].

The general principle of law laid down by the supreme court is applicable to every person including those who were not parties to the order [1996 11 SCC 261]. The right of the state to change its policy from time to time under the changing circumstances cannot be questioned though it may deviate from the judicial pronouncements of the supreme court [AIR 1998 SC 1703]. Parliament may by law confer on the Supreme court the power to issue directions.

1.4 India's New Criminal Laws (2024)

In a landmark reform of India's criminal justice system, three new laws came into force on 1 July 2024, replacing the colonial-era statutes that had governed Indian criminal law for over 160 years. These new laws are:

Bharatiya Nyaya Sanhita, 2023 (BNS) – replaces the Indian Penal Code (IPC), 1860. It has 358 sections (as against 511 in the IPC), introduces new offences such as organized crime and terrorism, and places greater focus on crimes against women and children.

Bharatiya Nagarik Suraksha Sanhita, 2023 (BNSS) – replaces the Code of Criminal Procedure (CrPC), 1973. It has 533 sections and introduces citizen-friendly procedural reforms, including Zero FIR (which allows filing an FIR at any police station regardless of jurisdiction), e-FIR filing online, defined timelines for investigation and trial, and forensic investigation as mandatory for serious offences.

Bharatiya Sakshya Adhiniyam, 2023 (BSA) – replaces the Indian Evidence Act (IEA), 1872. It has 170 sections and modernizes evidentiary law by recognizing electronic and digital records as primary evidence, and updates the framework for admissibility of forensic and scientific evidence.

These new laws apply to offences committed on or after 1 July 2024. Offences committed before that date continue to be governed by the old IPC and CrPC. Throughout this book, references to IPC sections or CrPC sections should be understood in this context: where a matter arises after 1 July 2024, the equivalent BNS or BNSS section will apply. Readers are encouraged to verify the corresponding section numbers in the BNS/BNSS/BSA when dealing with recent matters.

1.5 Conclusion

Understanding street law is the first step toward legal awareness in everyday life. It empowers individuals to protect their rights and navigate legal situations confidently. In the next chapter, we will explore how inheritance laws apply when a loved one passes away, ensuring that property and assets are distributed fairly and legally.

Chapter 2: What if my loved one has recently died leaving me property in their will : Inheritance Law

---

In this chapter, we discuss about inheritance law. This is applicable if a loved family member has recently died leaving us some property in their will.

THE INDIAN SUCCESSION ACT, 1925

ACT NO. 39 OF 1925[1]

[*30th September,* 1925.]

An Act to consolidate the law applicable to intestate and testamentary succession [2]***.

WHEREASit is expedient to consolidate the law applicable to intestate and testamentary succession [2]***. It is hereby enacted as follows:—

PART I

PRELIMINARY

1. Short title.—This Act may be called the Indian Succession Act, 1925.

2. Definitions.—In this Act, unless there is anything repugnant in the subject or context,—

(*a*) "administrator" means a person appointed by competent authority to administer the estate of a deceased person when there is no executor;

(*b*) "codicil" means an instrument made in relation to a Will, and explaining, altering or adding to its dispositions, and shall be deemed to form part of the Will;

[3][(*bb*) "District Judge" means the Judge of a Principal Civil Court of original jurisdiction;]

(*c*) "executor" means a person to whom the execution of the last Will of a deceased person is, by the testator's appointment, confided;

[4][(*cc*) "India" means the territory of India excluding the State of Jammu and Kashmir;]

(*d*) "Indian Christian" means a native of India who is, or in good faith claims to be, of unmixed Asiatic descent and who professes any form of the Christian religion;

Figure: First page of the Indian Succession Act 1925

2.1 Indian Succession Act 1925

The Indian Succession Act 1925 is an act to specify the law applicable to intestate (dying without a will) and testamentary succession (succession where a will is present). The law of succession is the law governing the transmission of property vested in a person at his death to some other person or persons.

2.2 Summary of the act

The Indian succession act covers different grounds related to wills and other aspects of succession.

It discusses who can and cannot make a will, what is a valid will, different types of bequests, how an administrator can be appointed, how probate and letters of succession can be granted, how debts, legacies and gifts are to be paid and so on. It also covers amendments made by the states.

2.3 Reasons for making a will

As per the act, if a person dies without making a will, the laws of the applicable state govern to whom their property should go to, depending on the closeness of family members and other relatives. However, if they have some preferences as to who should get their property and to what extent, it is better to make a will before one dies.

Other reasons to make a will include the following:

- To revoke any previous wills
- To identify any specific assets owned by one
- To appoint guardians or set up trusts for one's minor children
- To nominate executors and trustees to manage one's

assets

- To make gifts to individuals and charities and to provide for pets and servants
- To prevent family disputes about who gets what part of one's property
- To plan the distribution of one's estate so as to minimize taxes (such as inheritance tax and capital gains tax)
- To leave instructions about one's funeral rites, cremation or burial or how to dispose of one's body
- To donate one's organs, or one's entire body, for medical research or for organ transplants.

2.4 Characteristics of a will

The essential characteristics of a will are as follows:

- There must be a legal declaration of the testator's (the person making the will) intention
- The declaration must be with respect to the property of the testator
- The declaration must be to the effect that it is to operate after the death of the testator i.e., it must be revocable during the life of the testator.
- It lists the moveable and immoveable assets and states how and among whom the assets are to be divided and in what ratio
- The will must be signed and attested by two witnesses

The format of a simple will is as follows:

I, <name of testator>, son of <father's name>, aged <age in years>, resident of <address of testator>, declare this to be my last will and testament. This will cancels all my prior wills made by me.

I am in good health and possess a good mind. This will was made independently by me. No one has influenced or compelled me to make this will.

I hereby appoint <name of executor>, as the sole executor of this will.

My wife's name is <name of wife>. We have <number of children> children, whose names are as follows:

1.

2.

I have the following immovable and movable property:

1. A flat in the address _____

2. Jewelry, shares in various companies, cash and cash in bank accounts.

I declare that all the above assets are owned by me, and I have full authority over these assets.

I entrust all my movable and immovable properties to the following persons in the following ways

1. I give my bank account to my wife

2. I give my flat in the name of my son

( )

Testator's signature

Date

Signed by the testator as a last will in our presence. We have fully understood and approved the material and have signed our names as witnesses in the presence of the testator and in the presence of each other.

Name and signature of witnesses:

1.

2.

Declaration that this is the **last will** and previous wills are invalid
Declaration that the person is in good health and mind, and is making the will of their **own free choice**
Names of the **survivors** (wife and children etc.)
List of **moveable and immoveable property**
Description of **how the assets are to be divided**
Signature of the person with date
Names and Signatures of two witnesses

FIGURE: COMPONENTS of a will

2.5 How to find the will after a loved one's death

The following are the things to keep in mind for the legal heirs of the deceased, after the person's death:

- In some cases, a person may die suddenly and the family members may be uncertain about the existence of a will and ignorance to its location if it exists. In such a case, they may conclude the person left no will at all, but this may not be correct.

- Therefore, it is good to begin a search for a will as soon as possible after the death of the person.
- One common place to keep a will is the safe deposit box of a bank that is rented by the person who writes the will.
- If the will is not located in the safe deposit box, the next step may be to enquire from the person's bank if they have nominated any person as executor.
- If this too does not bring results, one may search the person's home, including his personal papers.
- Once a will has been found after a person's death, it should be opened and read. Then it should be acted upon, with the most immediate and urgent items acted first.

After finding the deceased's will, the legal heirs should apply for probate at the court, to obtain the authority to implement the terms named in the will.

If the deceased leaves a will which names executors, the executors must apply to the probate division of the high court for grant of probate.

2.6 COURT PROCEDURE for probating a will

The court procedure for probating a will generally include the following steps:

Submission: Petitioners submit probate application at the court in the prescribed format, along with death certificate, affidavit and court fees.

Verification: Court receives the probate application and verifies details.

Publication: Court directs to publish in newspapers a notice inviting members of the public and next of kin to file objections. It also directs to send notification letters to the next of kin.

Issuance: If there is no objection, the court issues the probate and letters of administration to the petitioners.

Upon Objection: If there is an objection, the normal court procedure takes place. After examining evidence and arguments, the court issues its judgment allowing or denying the grant of probate.

2.7 Conclusion

Knowing inheritance laws helps individuals claim their rightful property and avoid legal disputes. Understanding wills, succession laws, and probate procedures ensures a smooth transition of assets. Next, we will discuss tort law, which helps protect you from nuisances and trespassing, ensuring your property rights are respected.

Chapter 3: What if my neighbor is too noisy or trespassing on my property: Tort Law

---

If the neighbors are being too noisy or trespassing on our property, it typically comes under the terms of tort law.

3.1 Introduction to Tort Law

In criminal law, when someone commits a wrong, we call it a crime. Similarly, in civil law, when a person commits a wrong, we call it a tort. Typically, the wronged person files a case in a civil court to claim monetary or other damages from the wrong doer. The term "tort" is a French equivalent of the English word "wrong" and of the Roman law term "delict". The word is derived from the Latin word "tortum" which means an act which is twisted or crooked or wrong or unlawful.

3.2 Noisy neighbors: Tort of Nuisance

Nuisance as a tort means the unlawful interference with a person's use of enjoyment of land, or some right over or in connection with it.

The interference may be by any way such as noise, vibrations, heat, smoke, fumes, water, gas, electricity, excavations or disease producing germs.

For example, making loud noise in a normally quiet neighborhood at odd hours of the night may constitute a nuisance.

3.3 IPC laws on excessive noise

Excessive noise comes under public nuisance as defined in section 268 and the punishment is stated in section 290 of the Indian Penal Code (IPC). Section 268 is for causing annoyance to the public and can include, aside from noise, other kinds of annoyance such as threatening or denying public services to the public who lives in the area. Note: Under the Bharatiya Nyaya Sanhita (BNS), 2023, which replaced the IPC from 1 July 2024, public nuisance is covered under Section 292 of the BNS.

Section 268 of IPC on Public Nuisance states:

A person is guilty of a public nuisance who does any act or is guilty of an illegal omission which causes any common injury, danger or annoyance to the public or to the people in general who dwell or occupy property in the vicinity, or which must necessarily cause injury, obstruction, danger or annoyance to persons who may have occasion to use any public right. A common nuisance is not excused on the ground that it causes some convenience or advantage.

IPC Section 290 defines the punishment for causing public nuisance. It states as follows:

IPC 290 - Whoever commits a public nuisance in any case not otherwise punishable by this Code, shall be punished with fine which may extend to two hundred rupees.

Even though the amount of fine is negligible, the complaint might have the effect of dissuading the neighbor from repeating the loud noise in the future.

The Noise Pollution (Regulation and Control) Rules 2000 also have provisions against noise pollution. It limits one's neighbors from playing loud music, bursting loud firecrackers or making any sound on a loudspeaker that goes beyond a certain limit (usually 10 Decibels) over the ambient noise in that area in the nighttime.

Night time is defined between the times of 10 pm and 6 am in this act. However, this is relaxed till midnight for festive or cultural occasions such as Diwali or Independence Day.

The Noise Pollution Rules 2000 state the following:

(1) The noise levels in any area/zone shall not exceed the ambient air quality standards in respect of noise as specified in the Schedule. (2) The authority shall be responsible for the enforcement of noise pollution control measures and the due compliance of the ambient air quality standards in respect of noise.

So if the neighbors are making a loud noise and do not stop despite repeated warnings, one can call the police by dialing 100. A visit from the police is usually enough to get one's neighbors to stop the noise. However, if the problem still persists over a period of time, one can file a civil case as per tort law, along with documentation of previous complaints with the police.

3.4 Encroachment by Neighbors: Tort of Trespass

Trespass is an unlawful intrusion that interferes with a person or property. Specifically, it is a negligent or intentional act made by an individual that can cause injury to another person or their property without lawful justification, no matter how slight. It includes assault or threats made to a person, as well as trespass upon someone's property. The use of the term injury here means a violation of one's right and not actual physical harm or loss.

Trespass to property is one of the types of trespass. This includes trespass to chattels or moveable property as well as trespass to immoveable property. It typically applies to tangible property and allows the owners of such property to seek relief when a third party intentionally, carelessly or recklessly interferes or meddles with the owner's possession of such moveable or immoveable property.

Trespass to property is an act by someone where they don't have rights on one's property, yet they illegally occupy it without consent, or prevent the actual owner, from using it. This can be, for example, by installing gates, locks or other construction. In trespass, someone illegally enters or occupies property that legally belongs to someone else, against their will.

Trespass can be both civil and criminal. Criminal trespass is where the occupier threatens the owner of the property or commits assault on a person. Where criminal trespass does not apply, it is civil trespass and comes under tort law. Civil trespass leads to damages in civil court, while criminal trespass leads to criminal prosecution.

Section 441 of Indian Penal Code IPC deals with criminal trespass to property, and 447 for punishment for criminal trespass. Section 442 deals with house trespass. Note: Under the Bharatiya Nyaya Sanhita (BNS), 2023, which replaced the IPC from 1 July 2024, trespass is covered under Section 329 (criminal trespass) and Section 330 (house trespass).

Section 133 of IPC describes the procedure for removal of nuisances of illegal construction by neighbors.

The IPC laws on criminal and house trespass are as follows:

The IPC 441 states the following: *Whoever enters into or upon property in the possession of another with intent to commit an offence or to intimidate, insult or annoy any person in possession of such property, or having lawfully entered into or upon such property, unlawfully remains there with intent thereby to intimidate, insult or annoy any such person, or with intent to commit an offence, is said to commit "criminal trespass".*

IPC 442 states the following: *"Whoever commits criminal trespass by entering into or remaining in any building, tent or vessel used as a human dwelling or any building used as a place for worship, or as a place for the custody of property, is said to commit "house-trespass".*

If someone illegally occupies a part or whole of one's property, the following steps can be taken:

a. Obtain photos, videos and other proof of the trespassed property. If the person has made any illegal constructions on the property, get proof of that as well.

b. In case of criminal trespass or trespass with threats and intimidation, visit the nearest police station and/or file a written complaint, asking for help and protection. Include documentation and proofs such as photos.

c. Send a legal notice to the person who has trespassed, asking them to vacate the illegally trespassed property, failing which legal proceedings will be initiated.

d. File a lawsuit or writ petition before the courts (such as district court or high court) requesting direction to the police and other authorities for eviction of the occupier (neighbor who has trespassed) from the property and restoration of possession of that property to us.

e. File a suit before the courts requesting to pass an immediate stay / injunction against any construction and/or sale of the illegally occupied property, and demolishing of any illegal construction already made by the neighbor.

f. File a complaint to the municipal corporation (such as MCD in Delhi) against illegal trespass of our property by the neighbors, with proofs such as photos. This is also applicable if some construction has been made by the neighbors without proper planning permission.

g. File a written complaint before the sub divisional magistrate (SDM) with proofs.

h. File a civil suit for damages from the neighbors for illegal occupation of our property.

i. File a complaint with the revenue or land authorities to prevent mutation of land records by the neighbors.

3.5 Conclusion

Tort law provides legal remedies for wrongful acts like nuisance and trespassing. If your neighbor is being too noisy or unlawfully entering your property, legal actions can be taken. Moving forward, we will delve into contract law, which ensures fairness in agreements and protects consumers from unfair business practices.

Chapter 4: What if a company refuses to repair my mobile phone despite my having a warranty: Contract Law

In this chapter, we will discuss the concept of contracts and contract law in brief.

4.1 What is a contract

A contract is an agreement between two or more persons to exchange something of value. In a contract, each person is legally bound to do what is promised. A party who fails to live up to the agreed promise has breached the contract. When we agree to buy something, we essentially form a legal contract. The law of contract is relevant for many parts of our daily life, and it is important to understand contracts in order to protect ourselves as consumers.

In India, contract law is served by the Sale of Goods Act 1930 and by the Indian Contract Act 1872.

4.2 Meaning of contract

The meaning of contract, taken from different sources, is as follows:

- An agreement enforceable by law is a contract: Indian contract Act 1872

- An enforceable covenant or agreement between two or more persons with a lawful consideration or course (Tomlin)
- From dictionary of finance and investment: Contract in general is an agreement by which right or acts are exchanged for lawful consideration. to be valid, it must be entered into by competent parties, must cover a legal and moral transaction, must possess mutuality and must represent a meeting of moods. countless transactions in finance and investments are covered by contracts.
- While it is probably impossible to give an absolute and universally correct definition of a contract, the most accepted definition is a promise or a set of promises which the law will enforce. The expression "contract" may be used to describe any or all the following:

a. the series of promises or acts themselves constituting the contract

b. the document or documents constituting the contract

c. the document or documents constituting or evidencing that series or promises or acts or their performance

d. the legal relations resulting from that series

(Halisbury, 4th edition, Vol. 9, para 201, p80)

Contracts have been divided into three classes based on their function:

- Contracts of Record

- Contracts under seal
- Simple contracts

4.4 Indian Contract Act 1872

THE INDIAN CONTRACT ACT, 1872

ACT NO. 9 OF 1872[1]

[25th April, 1872.]

Preamble—WHEREAS it is expedient to define and amend certain parts of the law relating to contracts;

It is hereby enacted as follows:—

PRELIMINARY

1. Short title.—This Act may be called the Indian Contract Act, 1872.

Extent, Commencement.—It extends to the whole of India [2][except the State of Jammu and Kashmir]; and it shall come into force on the first day of September, 1872.

Saving—[3]*** Nothing herein contained shall affect the provisions of any Statute, Act or Regulation not hereby expressly repealed, nor any usage or custom of trade, nor any incident of any contract, not inconsistent with the provisions of this Act.

2. Interpretation-clause.—In this Act the following words and expressions are used in the following senses, unless a contrary intention appears from the context:—

(*a*) When one person signifies to another his willingness to do or to abstain from doing anything, with a view to obtaining the assent of that other to such act or abstinence, he is said to make a proposal;

---

1. For the Statement of Objects and Reasons for the Bill which was based on a a report of Her Majesty's Commissioners appointed to prepare a body of substantive law for India, dated 6th July, 1866, see Gazette of India, 1867 Extraordinary, p. 34; for

Figure: First page of the Indian Contract Act 1872

The Indian Contract Act 1872 is the main act that defines the contract law in India. It states the circumstances in which a contract between two or more parties can be enforced in Indian law.

4.5 Elements of a Contract as per Indian Contract Act 1872

A legally binding contract must have the following elements, as per the Indian contract act 1872:

- **Offer**: There must be an offer by one party
- **Acceptance**: The offer must be accepted by another party. The law infers acceptance from certain actions, such as signing a contact or beginning to carry out the terms of a bargain.
- **Promise**: When the offer is accepted, it becomes a promise, which is legally enforceable.
- **Promisor and Promisee**: The person who makes the promise is called the promisor. The promise must be directed to a specific person, who accepts the promise and is called the promisee.
- **Consideration**: This refers to the price paid for the promise. In every valid contract, there must be an exchange of consideration. this means that something of value is given for something else of value. For example, if you buy a blouse at a store, your consideration is the money being paid and the merchant's consideration is the item being bought. The value of the two items does not have to be the same, and law allows consumers to make both good deals and bad deals.
- **Agreement**: The promises made along with the consideration for the promise is called the agreement.
- **Contract**: An agreement enforceable by law is a contract.
- **Void contract**: A void contract is a contract that is not enforceable by law
- People entering into a contract must be legally competent to make contracts. For example, they cannot be mentally ill or intoxicated, or less than the

minimum age for contracts.

4.6 Acceptance, lawful consideration and competent persons as per the Indian Contract Act

The rules for acceptance of a contract as per the Indian Contract Act 1930 are as follows:

- **Absolute and unqualified**: Acceptance of an offer by a party should be absolute and unqualified. For example, there should not be a counteroffer by the party to buy the items at a different price than that one offered
- **Communicated**: The acceptance should be communicated to the party making the offer, in a written or verbal form.
- **Mode**: Acceptance must be in the mode prescribed. If not, the offerer may inform the same to the person accepting the offer that the acceptance is not as per the prescribed mode such as writing or verbal or email.
- **Time frame**: The acceptance must be made within a specific time frame and before the offer is lapsed.
- **Acceptance after offer**: The acceptance can only be after an offer is made, not earlier.
- Silence by one party cannot be held as acceptance

The rules for lawful consideration as per the Indian Contract Act include the following:

- The action should be at the desire or request of the

promisor. If the action has been made without the promisor expressly requesting for it, then no consideration is payable.

- The consideration must be real and having some value as per law.
- Consideration may be in the past, present or future.
- Consideration may move from the promisee to another person.
- Consideration need not be adequate or equal in value.
- Consideration must not be something that the promiser is already bound to do.
- Consideration should not be forbidden by law
- Consideration should not involve injury to any person
- Consideration should not be immoral, fraudulent, or opposed to public policy

The persons competent to make a contract include the following:

- The person should not be a minor
- They should not be of unsound mind when making the contract, such as mentally ill or intoxicated
- They should not be disqualified by law from making the contract, such as being a convict, or alien enemy.
- They should be making the contract out of their own free will and consent, and not be subject to coercion, undue influence, fraud or misrepresentation.

4.7 Invalid and unenforceable contracts

Agreements to do something illegal or something that is against public policy are not enforceable in the courts. For example, an agreement to sell illegal drugs.

A minor person usually cannot enter into a contract. E.g., a person under the age of 18 for male and 21 for female is a minor and cannot enter into a contract.

A contract that is unfair e.g., which favors a particular party may be found unfair and unconscionable, and hence unenforceable in the court if the following conditions are met:

- the consumer is presented with a contract on a take it or leave it basis.
- there is uneven bargaining power between the parties, such as when the seller is educated and experienced and the consumer is uneducated.

Some types of work bonds, such as a promise to work in an IT company for a certain number of years or to never work for a competitor, may also be unenforceable.

Fraud and misrepresentation are grounds for invalidating a contract. An example of a fraud is a false statement to induce one party to agree to a contract. Misrepresentation can be in the form of either making a misleading statement or intentionally withholding information in a statement that could have caused the party to not agree to the contract.

4.8 Warranty

Warranty is a type of contract, or one or more conditions present in a contract. A warranty is a promise or guarantee made by a seller concerning the quality or performance of goods offered for sale. It is usually valid for a limited time period. A warranty is a statement of what the seller will do to fix any defect in the product, or if it does not perform as advertised, within the time period of its validity. If the seller does not honor the warranty, the contract is said to be breached.

The sale of goods act 1930 states the flowing:

13. When condition to be treated as warranty.—

(1) Where a contract of sale is subject to any condition to be fulfilled by the seller, the buyer may waive the condition or elect to treat the breach of the condition as a breach of warranty and not as a ground for treating the contract as repudiated.

(2) Where a contract of sale is not severable and the buyer has accepted the goods or part thereof, the breach of any condition to be fulfilled by the seller can only be treated as a breach of warranty and not as a ground for rejecting the goods and treating the contract as repudiated, unless there is a term of the contract, express or implied, to that effect.

(3) Nothing in this section shall affect the case of any condition or warranty fulfilment of which is excused by law by reason of impossibility or otherwise.

There are two types of warranties: express and implied.

- Express warranty: it is an express statement

concerning the quality or performance of goods for sale that is part of the contract of sale.

- Implied warranty: this is understood by the conduct of the seller to the buyer of the goods.

In the following section, we look at another law in India related to contracts for sale of goods.

4.9 Sale of Goods Act 1930

In this section, we go through the Sale of Goods Act of 1930, which defines the law related to the sale of goods and transfer of ownership, including moveable property but not land. It mainly focuses on contracts between the buyers and sellers.

THE SALE OF GOODS ACT, 1930

ACT NO. 3 OF 1930[1]

[15th March, 1930.]

An Act to define and amend the law relating to the sale of goods.

WHEREAS it is expedient to define and amend the law relating to the sale of goods; It is hereby enacted as follows:—

CHAPTER I

PRELIMINARY

1. **Short title, extent and commencement.**—(1) This Act may be called the [2]*** Sale of Goods Act, 1930.

[3][(2) It extends to the whole of India [4][except the State of Jammu and Kashmir].]

(3) It shall come into force on the 1st day of July, 1930.

2. **Definitions.**—In this Act, unless there is anything repugnant in the subject or context,—

(1) "buyer" means a person who buys or agrees to buy goods;

(2) "delivery" means voluntary transfer of possession from one person to another;

(3) goods are said to be in a "deliverable state" when they are in such state that the buyer would under the contract be bound to take delivery of them;

(4) "document of title to goods" includes a bill of lading, dockwarrant, warehouse keeper's certificate, wharfingers' certificate, railway receipt, [5][multimodal transport document,] warrant or order for the delivery of goods and any other document used in the ordinary course of business as proof of the possession or control of goods, or authorising or purporting to authorise, either by endorsement or by delivery, the possessor of the document to transfer or receive goods thereby

Figure: First page of the Sale of Goods Act 1930

The Sale of Goods Act 1930 defines a contract for a sale of goods between a buyer and a seller, where the ownership of an item is transferred from the seller to the buyer upon payment of a price. The term goods refers to "every kind of movable property other than actionable claims and money; and includes stock and shares, growing crops, grass, and things attached to or forming part of the land which are agreed to be severed before sale or under the contract of sale."

Along with the ownership and rights, any risks and liabilities associated with the item are also transferred from the seller to the buyer. the act covers existing goods as well as goods to be transferred in the future.

The Sale of Goods act defines what is a contract of sale and the various conditions associated with the contract. It also covers various cases where the goods are faulty or the contract conditions are not met. It covers the rights of the buyers and the sellers, as well as special conditions like damaged goods and auctions.

4.10 Conclusion

Contracts govern everyday transactions, from buying a phone to signing a job agreement. Understanding contract law helps in enforcing warranties and protecting consumer rights. In the next chapter, we will explore laws against discrimination in the workplace, ensuring equal treatment and protection under the law.

Chapter 5: What if I am discriminated against in my job: Law of Discrimination

---

5.1 What is discrimination

Discrimination occurs when some people are treated differently than others due to their membership in a group, such as their race, gender, age or religion.

Examples of discrimination are as follows: a landlord may not give their house on rent to people of a certain religion or caste. A company may pay different salaries to male and female employees doing the same work.

Figure: Screenshot of articles 14 and 15 of the Indian Constitution

5.2 Section 15 of Indian Constitution

Section 15 of the Indian constitution bans discrimination on the basis of sex, religion, race, caste or place of birth. It follows and qualifies section 14 stating the right to equality.

Discrimination may be both positive and negative. Positive discrimination refers to treating a specific community positively, while negative discrimination refers to denying opportunities to people having a specific trait or belonging to a specific community.

However, all discrimination is not illegal. The article 15 of the Constitution itself mentions that the state can make special provisions for the social and educational advancement of certain sections of society such as scheduled castes and tribes, or women.

5.3 High Court View of Discrimination in Pay

The High Court in a recent judgment took the view that retrospective bifurcation of pay scales earlier existing common cadre of junior engineers with effect from 3.7.1969 was bad and that decision having remained unchallenged had become final. This means that on a parity of reasoning and as a logical corollary it must follow that bifurcation of pay scales of all common cadre retrospectively is bad, else the position would be inconsistent. Same goes for discrimination in terms of the policy of benefit of encashment of half day leaves for different classes of employees.

5.4 Examples of cases held discriminatory by Indian courts

Some examples include the following:

- Infliction of punishment by the appellate authority acting as a disciplinary authority is discriminatory as it denies the right to appeal [AIR 1995 SC 1053].
- Denying grants in aid to government recognized private law colleges while extending such benefits to recognized private colleges with other facilities is discriminatory [AIR 1996 SC 1201].
- The grant of special remission to prisoners of scheduled castes and scheduled tribes and the denial of the same to other prisoners is discriminatory. However, the grant of such remission itself was deemed unlawful [AIR 1996 SC 2106].
- Where the entire selection process was found to be illegal and the selection was squashed, protecting the candidates who had received training and were appointed under the interim order of the high court [1995 Supp (1) SCC 266].

5.4 Examples of cases held non-discriminatory by Indian courts

Some examples include the following:

- Concessional tariff of electricity to agriculturists and not to industrial consumers is non-discriminatory, as the former is a separate class [AIR 1995 SC 2234].
- Procedure for trial prescribed by the parliament for deciding cases under TADA act is held non-discriminatory as no discretionary option is left to the

state government for choosing the procedure for trial [AIR 1996 SC 3305].

- Denial of illegal benefit to others similarly situated was held to be non-discriminatory [AIR 2000 SC 2306].

- Paying the same price of sugarcane to growers of the zone - to both members of cooperative societies and no the non-members, was held as non-discriminatory.

- Denying reservation to the other backward classes while reserving posts for scheduled castes and scheduled tribes is held as non-discriminatory. [1995 Supp (3) SCC 475]

5.5 How the Courts Determine if Discrimination has Occurred

The Constitution of India provides that the state shall not deny to any person the equal protection of the law. To determine whether a law or government practice meets the equal protection standard, courts use three different tests depending on the type of discrimination involved:

- **The Reasonable Basis Test**: This test is used in most discrimination cases. Using this test, the judges will upload the law or practice involved if it has a reasonable basis i.e. where there is a logical relationship between the classification and purpose of the law.

- **The Strict Scrutiny Test**: This test is used when certain laws or practices discriminate on the basis of race, national origin, citizenship status, or some fundamental right in the Indian constitution such as freedom of religion. Judges applying strict scrutiny will find the law or practice unconstitutional unless the state can show that it serves a compelling interest and that there is no less intrusive way to satisfy that interest. For example, this test was used in Saurabh Chaudhary & Ors v. Union of India to determine whether reservation based on domicile or institutional preference is unconstitutional.

- **The Substantial Relationship Test**: In sex discrimination cases, the Supreme Court may use the substantial relationship test. In these cases, there must be a close connection (not just a rational relationship) between the law or practice and its purpose. In addition, laws that differ based on sex must serve an important governmental purpose.

5.6 Conclusion

Discrimination laws safeguard individuals from unfair treatment based on gender, caste, religion, or disability. Legal provisions ensure workplace equality and fair pay. Next, we will discuss the law of credit, helping you understand loans, credit cards, and how to protect yourself from financial fraud.

Chapter 6: What if I Need to Take a Loan: Law of Credit

Using credit means buying goods or services now in exchange for a promise to pay sometime in the future. It also means borrowing money now in exchange for a promise to repay it in the future.

People who lend money or provide credit are called creditors, and those who borrow money or receive credit are called debtors. Debtors usually pay the creditors interest, finance charges or an additional money over the sum borrowed, for the privilege of using the credit.

6.1 Types of credit

There are two main types of credit: unsecured and secured.

In **secured credit**, the borrower has to pledge some property of value, called collateral, in order to obtain the credit. Collateral is a protection against the possibility that the credit is not repaid. If the borrower does not keep up with the repayments and defaults on the loan, the lender can take the collateral. An example of a secured credit is a housing loan from the bank, in which the house registration documents have to be kept with the bank as collateral.

In **unsecured credit**, the promise is enough and there is no need to pledge property. Credit cards are examples of unsecured credit.

6.2 Bank Loans

Bank loans may be provided to customers in a bank to enable them to finance the purchase of a house or car or foreign studies etc. These loans may be repayable over a fixed amount of time, such as 10 or 15 years.

These bank loans are subject to a credit check by the bank and credit agencies, to determine the credit-worthiness of the customer, before the loan is approved. The bank may require other documents such as salary slips to determine how much the customer would be able to repay the loan. Interest is payable on the bank loans at a rate that could be either fixed or variable.

There may be clauses about penalties for early closure of the loan. Also, if regular repayments for the loan are not maintained, the credit rating may be affected adversely.

6.3 Credit Cards

Many companies including banks use credit cards. They can be used in a variety of purposes such as buying fuel from petrol stations or buying goods such as electronics or clothes in a physical shop or online e-commerce portal.

Credit cards are engraved with the holder's name, CVC code, card number, name of bank, and are usually embedded with a machine-readable chip. Some banks charge a fixed amount per year for the card, others may provide it for free. The interest rate for the credit may vary from card to card. There may be special offers or points associated with the usage of specific types of cards for specific purposes. For example, a store may provide certain points if a credit card is used to buy from amazon.com.

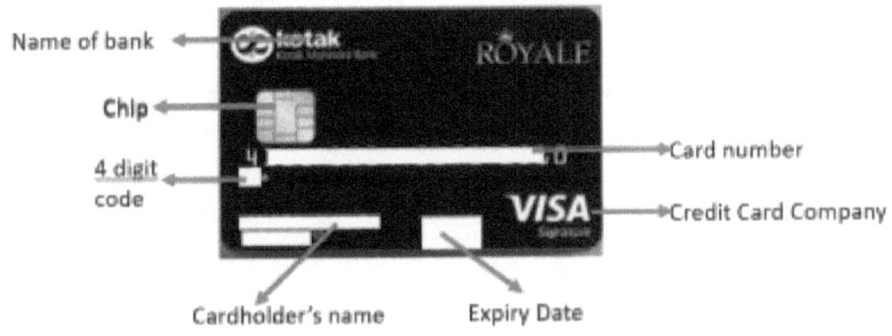

Figure: An example credit card showing the elements of the card.

Credit card companies usually send out monthly statements indicating the amount spent and how much is the minimum repayment expected for that month. If the customer does not make the minimum payment, their credit rating might be affected, and an additional fine may be charged.

Credit cards are a convenient way for customers to pay their monthly bills. Often, they have repayment options that allow repayment of a large debt, such as on purchase of a fridge or Apple iphone, spread over easy monthly installments. However, the interest on a credit card can be high and it is worthwhile to pay more than the minimum repayment on the credit card each month to avoid having to pay a huge sum as interest.

6.4 Conclusion

Credit laws protect borrowers from unfair lending practices and help them make informed financial decisions. Understanding loan agreements and credit card terms can prevent financial troubles. Next, we will discuss marriage laws, covering the legal aspects of marriage registration and rights of spouses.

Chapter 7: How to Register a Marriage: Law of Marriage

In order to register a marriage, we have to follow the conditions for a valid marriage as per the Hindu Marriage Act or Special Marriage Act.

7.1 Laws Related to Marriage in India

The main laws related to marriages in India are as follows:

Hindu Marriage Act 1955: The Hindu Marriage Act 1955 governs marriage between a Hindu man and woman, conducted as per Hindu rites. This definition also includes Sikhs, Jains and Buddhists.

Special Marriage Act 1954: The Special Marriage Act 1954 covers marriages between any two citizens of India, regardless of their religion and including inter-religious marriages. It does not specify any particular rites for the marriage.

Conditions for a valid marriage as per the Hindu Marriage Act are as follows:

- The bride and groom should be above the legal minimum age (21 years for groom and 18 for bride)
- The marriage must be solemnized in accordance with the customary rites and ceremonies of either party and where such rites and ceremonies include "Saptapadi" (taking the seven steps together by bride

and groom before the sacred fire), that requirement must be observed. Note that the same requirement is not applicable in the special marriage act.

- There should not be a subsisting valid marriage of either of the parties with any other person.
- The parties should, as regards age and mental capacity, be competent to have a marriage solemnized between them.
- The parties should not by reason of degrees of prohibited relationship or "sapinda" relationship be debarred from marrying one another. This includes, for example, marriage between cousins.

If any of the above conditions are not met, the marriage can be declared void.

There are a few additional conditions that render a marriage invalid

- Impotency of any of the parties
- Mental incapacity of the party at the time of the marriage
- That the consent of the party or the guardian had been obtained by force or fraud
- The person was at the time of the marriage pregnant by some person other than the petitioner and the petitioner was at the time of the marriage ignorant of the fact

7.2 Registration of a marriage

For registration of a marriage, as per the above acts, the parties have to approach the registrar in their city with required documents including wedding invitation card, wedding photo, ID and address proof of both parties and a filled application form.

After the registrar verifies all the documents in the presence of the parties, he issues the marriage registration certificate.

7.3 Conclusion

Marriage laws define the legal process of marriage registration and the rights and responsibilities of spouses. Understanding these laws helps protect individuals in marital relationships. In the next chapter, we will explore labor law, ensuring protection against unfair dismissal and workplace exploitation.

Chapter 8: What if I am Fired Unfairly from my Job: Labor Law

If an employee is fired unfairly from their job, they can file a complaint with the labor commissioner or assistant labor commissioner of the state. One can also file a lawsuit against one's employer in the court. Unjust firing falls under the applicable labor laws.

8.1 What are Labor Laws

Labor laws govern the conditions for initiation of employment, conditions of work, industrial action or strikes, unions, as well as dismissal from employment.

The main labor laws in India include the following:

- Industrial Disputes Act, 1947
- The Workmen's Compensation Act, 1923
- State Shops and Establishments Act
- Unorganized Workers' Social Security Act, 2008, which covers domestic workers.

The Indian government has enacted a new set of labour codes to consolidate and simplify the existing labour laws. These four codes were passed by Parliament but their implementation has been deferred pending state-level rules notification. As of 2025, they have not yet come into force. These are the following:

- Code of Wages, 2019
- Industrial Relations Code, 2020
- Occupational Safety, Health and Working Conditions Code 2020
- Code on Social Security, 2020

8.2 Unfair Dismissal

Unfair dismissal or termination of employment is where an employer terminates the employment of an employee without giving a string and valid reason.

As per the **Industrial Relations Code 2020**, termination of employment for any reason other than disciplinary action comes under retrenchment. This requires a month's written notice period on part of the employer, along with 15 days of average pay as compensation for every year of active service with that employer.

Some employers, to avoid paying the compensation and other legal steps, try to force the employees to resign. However, forced resignation is not valid as per the labor laws. In case a number of employees have been forced to resign, the group of employees can together approach the labor commissioner. They can also approach the labor unions, if they exist, for assistance and advice. They can also approach the courts.

In addition, if the employee feels they have been discriminated in their termination from work, they can approach the courts for compensation for discrimination as well.

MINISTRY OF LAW AND JUSTICE
(Legislative Department)

New Delhi, the 29th September, 2020/Asvina 7, 1942 (Saka)

The following Act of Parliament received the assent of the President on the 28th September, 2020 and is hereby published for general information:—

THE INDUSTRIAL RELATIONS CODE, 2020

No. 35 OF 2020

[28th September, 2020.]

An Act to consolidate and amend the laws relating to Trade Unions, conditions of employment in industrial establishment or undertaking, investigation and settlement of industrial disputes and for matters connected therewith or incidental thereto.

BE it enacted by Parliament in the Seventy-first Year of the Republic of India as follows:—

CHAPTER I

PRELIMINARY

1. (*1*) This Act may be called the Industrial Relations Code, 2020.

(*2*) It shall extend to the whole of India.

(*3*) It shall come into force on such date as the Central Government may, by notification in the Official Gazette appoint; and different dates may be appointed for different provisions of this Code and any reference in any such provision to the commencement of this Code shall be construed as a reference to the coming into force of that provision.

Figure: First page of the Industrial Relations Code 2020

8.3 Industrial Relations Code 2020

The code states the following provisions related to layoffs and retrenchments:

"retrenchment" means the termination by the employer of the service of a worker for any reason whatsoever, otherwise than as a punishment inflicted by way of disciplinary action,

No worker employed in any industry who has been in continuous service for not less than one year under an employer shall be retrenched by that employer until—

(a) the worker has been given one month's notice in writing indicating the reasons for retrenchment and the period of notice has expired, or the worker has been paid in lieu of such notice, wages for the period of the notice;

(b) the worker has been paid, at the time of retrenchment, compensation which shall be equivalent to fifteen days' average pay, or average pay of such days as may be notified by the appropriate Government, for every completed year of continuous service or any part thereof in excess of six months; and

(c) notice in such manner as may be prescribed is served on the appropriate Government or such authority as may be specified by the appropriate Government by notification.

67. Whenever a worker (other than a badli worker or a casual worker) whose name is borne on the muster rolls of an industrial establishment and who has completed not less than one year of continuous service under an employer is laid-off, whether continuously or intermittently, he shall be paid by the employer for all days during which he is so laid-off, except for such weekly holidays as may intervene, compensation which shall be equal to fifty per cent. of the total of the basic wages and dearness allowance that would have been payable to him, had he not been so laid-off:

Provided that if during any period of twelve months, a worker is so laid-off for more than forty-five days, no such compensation shall be payable in respect of any period of the lay-off after the expiry of the first forty-five days, if there is an agreement to that effect between the worker and the employer:

Provided further that it shall be lawful for the employer in any case falling within the foregoing proviso to retrench the worker in accordance with the provisions contained in section 70 at any time after the expiry of the first forty-five days of the lay-off and when he does so, any compensation paid to the worker for having been laid-off during the preceding twelve months may be set off against the compensation payable for retrenchment.

8.4 Conclusion

Labor laws protect employees from unfair termination and ensure workplace rights are upheld. Knowing these laws can help employees fight wrongful dismissal. Next, we will discuss defamation laws, which help individuals protect their reputation from false accusations and misleading statements.

Chapter 9: What if Someone Tries to Defame me: Law of Defamation

In this chapter we discuss the Indian law on defamation. We can use this to protect our reputation in case someone makes defamatory or slanderous statements against us.

9.1 What is Defamation

A defamatory statement or defamation is one which harms the reputation of a person by exposing them to hatred, contempt or ridicule, which tends to reduce the respect of members of the society towards that person or induce hostility towards them. It can be in written or spoken form. It is usually intentional, i.e. done with the intent to malign the person's reputation.

Article 19(1) of the Indian constitution protects the freedom of speech and the right of citizens of India to express their views freely. However this right is subject to restrictions such as in case of defamatory statements. The article 19(2) states as follows:

(2) Nothing in sub clause (a) of clause (1) shall affect the operation of any existing law, or prevent the State from making any law, in so far as such law imposes reasonable restrictions on the exercise of the right conferred by the said sub clause in the interests of the sovereignty and integrity of India, the security of the State, friendly relations with foreign States, public order,

decency or morality or in relation to contempt of court, defamation or incitement to an offence

The law on defamation in India seeks to drive a balance between the constitutional protected right to free speech and the need to protect a person's reputation from harm.

9.2 Types of Defamation

There are two types of defamation which are as follows:

Libel: it is the publication of a defamatory statement in some permanent form, such as writing or printing an article in a newspaper or sharing in social media.

Slander: it is the publication of a defamatory statement in a transient and temporary form, such as by spoken words.

In English law, these are treated differently. However, the laws for both types of defamation are the same in India: both libel and slander are criminal offenses.

9.3 Conditions of Defamation

The following are the conditions to prove to the court that defamation has occurred in India:

- There must be a defamatory statement that is made
- The said statement must be about a person or a specific group of persons, not to a broad class of people
- The statement must be published in oral or written form and accessible by a third person

In addition, the following conditions are generally needed before a defamation suit can be successful:

- The statement should be defamatory in nature e.g. which can harm the reputation
- The statement must be untrue
- The statement should be made with a malicious intention
- The statement must cause harm to the reputation of the plaintiff or some other harm, such as cause them to lose their job or lose customer sales in their business.
- The statement should not be made by a member of parliament or other privileged person. In India, MPs during discussion in parliament and some other privileged persons are protected from defamation lawsuits.

The defendant, i.e. the person who is alleged to make the defamatory statement, can defend themselves by proving that the statement was true, or that it was made in public interest in good faith based on a true incident.

9.4 Burden of proof in a suit of defamation

In case a defamation suit is brought in the court, the burden of proof lies on the plaintiff, i.e. the person who has filed the lawsuit in the court. They have to prove that the statement made was untrue and caused harm to them in some way.

9.5 IPC Sections for Criminal Defamation in India

As with most other types of tort, defamation comes under both civil law and criminal law in India. As in all cases, for a criminal offence, the burden of proof is higher and has to be beyond all reasonable doubt, while for the civil case it is only to be proved on the balance of probabilities that defamation has occurred.

Under criminal law, defamation comes under sections 499 and 500 of the Indian Penal Code or IPC. The defamed person can file a criminal case for defamation in court. Intentional act of defamation is punishable by imprisonment as defined in Section 500 of the IPC. Note: Under the Bharatiya Nyaya Sanhita (BNS), 2023, which replaced the IPC with effect from 1 July 2024, defamation is now covered under Section 356 of the BNS. For offences committed on or after 1 July 2024, Section 356 of BNS applies instead of IPC Sections 499 and 500.

Defamation is a bailable, non-cognizable and compoundable offence under the IPC.

The IPC sections are as follows:

499. Defamation.—Whoever, by words either spoken or intended to be read, or by signs or by visible representations, makes or publishes any imputation concerning any person intending to harm, or knowing or having reason to believe that such imputation will harm, the reputation of such person, is said, except in the cases hereinafter expected, to defame that person.

Explanation 1.—It may amount to defamation to impute anything to a deceased person, if the imputation would harm the reputation of that person if living, and is intended to be hurtful to the feelings of his family or other near relatives.

Explanation 2.—It may amount to defamation to make an imputation concerning a company or an association or collection of persons as such.

Explanation 3.—An imputation in the form of an alternative or expressed ironically, may amount to defamation.

Explanation 4.—No imputation is said to harm a person's reputation, unless that imputation directly or indirectly, in the estimation of others, lowers the moral or intellectual character of that person, or lowers the character of that person in respect of his caste or of his calling, or lowers the credit of that person, or causes it to be believed that the body of that person is in a loathsome state, or in a state generally considered as disgraceful.

The IPC section 500 defines the punishment for criminal defamation.

500. Punishment for defamation.—Whoever defames another shall be punished with simple imprisonment for a term which may extend to two years, or with fine, or with both.

9.6 Procedure for Civil Defamation

For a civil defamation lawsuit, the normal court procedure takes place. It involves filing the case in the court, sending notice to the defendant, presentation of witnesses, arguments by both parties and the final judgment or verdict of the court.

9.7 Conclusion

Defamation laws protect individuals from false statements that harm their reputation. Understanding libel and slander helps in taking legal action against defamation. Moving forward, we will discuss perjury laws, which address false statements made in court and their legal consequences.

Chapter 10: What if Someone Makes a False Statement in Court: Law of Perjury

In this chapter we discuss the Indian law on perjury.

10.1 Definition of Perjury

Perjury is the offense of knowingly lying to the court, or intentionally giving a false or misleading statement to the court, whether as an oral statement or declaration given under oath or a written statement in an affidavit or used as evidence in a court case. The statement should be one that is known to be false by the person at that time.

As per the Merriam Webster dictionary, perjury is "the voluntary violation of an oath or vow either by swearing to what is untrue or by omission to do what has been promised under oath : false swearing". As per Encyclopedia Britannica, perjury in law is "the giving of false testimony under oath on an issue or point of inquiry regarded as material."

Since the court system in India and other countries relies on testimony of witnesses and others, therefore false testimony has the effect of undermining the justice system and preventing justice. There have been numerous situations in the past where witnesses in cases turned hostile or gave false testimony, which is why the law to tackle perjury is important.

10.2 Indian law related to perjury

As per Indian law, perjury is not a crime per se as per Indian Penal Code or IPC, however, false evidence is a crime and is covered under section 191 of IPC, which states the following: "*Giving false evidence.—Whoever, being legally bound by an oath or by an express provision of law to state the truth, or being bound by law to make a declaration upon any subject, makes any statement which is false, and which he either knows or believes to be false or does not believe to be true, is said to give false evidence.*"

The punishment for false evidence is defined as per section 193 of IPC. It states the following: "*Whoever intentionally gives false evidence in any of a judicial proceeding, or fabricates false evidence for the purpose of being used in any stage of a judicial proceeding, shall be punished with imprisonment of either description for a term which may extend to seven years, and shall also be liable to fine; and whoever intentionally gives or fabricates false evidence in any other case, shall be punished with imprisonment of either description for a term which may extend to three years, and shall also be liable to fine.*"

Sections 340 and 195 of the Code of Criminal Procedure or CRPC refer to the procedure to be followed by the court to determine if perjury has occurred and should be persecuted. Section 195 of the CRPC lays down rules to be followed by the court to decide whether any prosecution is necessary or not for the offense alleged under it, and section 340 lays down the steps for the court to initiate prosecution as per section 195. Note: With the coming into force of the Bharatiya Nagarik Suraksha Sanhita (BNSS) on 1 July 2024, the equivalent provisions are found in Sections 223 and 340 of the BNSS for offences occurring after that date.

10.3 Procedure for filing a perjury application

Perjury proceedings are started when some person gives a complaint in form of an affidavit alleging perjury by one or more persons to the court, along with the evidence on which the complaint is based. The person filing the perjury complaint can be either a party to the court case in which the perjury has occurred, or else it can also be filed by any interested person.

The court has to investigate whether an inquiry should be made and whether to persecute or not. In particular, one of the conditions for sanctioning prosecution is that it is not to be used as a means for taking revenge. The court has to decide whether it wishes to initiate persecution or not, in the interests of justice.

10.4 False complaint of perjury

If however, the complaint of perjury is found to be false and malicious, proceedings can be started against the person who gave the false complaint of perjury under section 211 of the Indian penal code (Section 250 of BNS for matters after 1 July 2024).

The section 211 states "*False charge of offence made with intent to injure.—Whoever, with intent to cause injury to any person, institutes or causes to be instituted any criminal proceeding against that person, or falsely charges any person with having committed an offence, knowing that there is no just or lawful ground for such proceeding or charge against that person, shall be punished with imprisonment of either description for a term which may extend to two years, or with fine, or with both."*

10.5 Conclusion

Perjury laws ensure the integrity of the legal system by punishing false statements in court. Knowing the consequences of perjury can help individuals make truthful declarations. Next, we will explore the Right to Information (RTI) law, which empowers citizens to seek transparency from government bodies.

Chapter 11: Transparency: Right to Information Law

Every citizen of India has the right to ask the government at center and state level about any information pertaining to data of any of the government departments. This is called RTI or Right to information. This act has become an essential tool for citizens to facilitate transparency of the government departments and curb corruption.

In this chapter, we go through the RTI Act and the steps to file an RTI.

11.1 Introduction to RTI Act

The Right to Information (RTI) Bill was passed in 2005 in the Indian parliament. It covers most public offices in the government, except for a few such as defense. Citizens can query for any information related to any of the public offices or government departments, and the department has to reply within a fixed time which is usually 30 days. However, the judiciary, political parties and private offices are not covered under the act.

As per the act, certain information can be denied if it pertains to the life and liberty of a person, are related to trade secrets or would compromise the integrity and security of the nation, for example related to defense related confidential information.

As per the act, a post of Chief information commissioner (CIC) is appointed at the central level and Public information officers (PIO) are appointed at the state level to oversee the RTIs.

सूचना का अधिकार अधिनियम, 2005

(2005 का अधिनियम संख्यांक 22)

[1 फरवरी, 2011 को यथाविद्यमान]

Right to Information Act, 2005

(Act No. 22 of 2005)

[*As modified up to 1st February, 2011*]

Figure: First Page of the RTI Act

Section 6 of the RTI Act states as follows:

6. Request for obtaining information.—

(1) A person, who desires to obtain any information under this Act, shall make a request in writing or through electronic means

in English or Hindi in the official language of the area in which the application is being made, accompanying such fee as may be prescribed, to—

(a) the Central Public Information Officer or State Public Information Officer, as the case may be, of the concerned public authority;

(b) the Central Assistant Public Information Officer or State Assistant Public Information Officer, as the case may be, specifying the particulars of the information sought by him or her: Provided that where such request cannot be made in writing, the Central Public Information Officer or State Public Information Officer, as the case may be, shall render all reasonable assistance to the person making the request orally to reduce the same in writing.

(2) An applicant making request for information shall not be required to give any reason for requesting the information or any other personal details except those that may be necessary for contacting him.

(3) Where an application is made to a public authority requesting for an information,—

(i) which is held by another public authority; or

(ii) the subject matter of which is more closely connected with the functions of another public authority, the public authority, to which such application is made, shall transfer the application or such part of it as may be appropriate to that other public authority and inform the applicant immediately about such transfer: Provided that the transfer of an application pursuant to this

sub-section shall be made as soon as practicable but in no case later than five days from the date of receipt of the application.

11.2 Process for filing an RTI

The RTI process includes the following:

1. The citizen files an RTI request either online or by postal mail to the central or state government department concerned, paying the required fees (nominal charges of Rs 10) and submitting the necessary documents.

2. The query or request for information goes to the Comissioner or public information officer of the state or center depending on whom the RTI has been requested, who then forwards the query to the concerned department.

3. The department has to submit a reply to the citizen's query within 30 days.

4. There is also appeals process as part of the RTI. The citizen can file an appeal in the prescribed form if the reply received is not satisfactory.

11.3 How to file an RTI Request

One needs to go to the RTI portal for the central government or the state.

The central government RTI portal is https://www.rtionline.gov.in/

Nowadays many third party tools and websites are also available that will fill an RTI request for you on payment of a small fee and filling the details online.

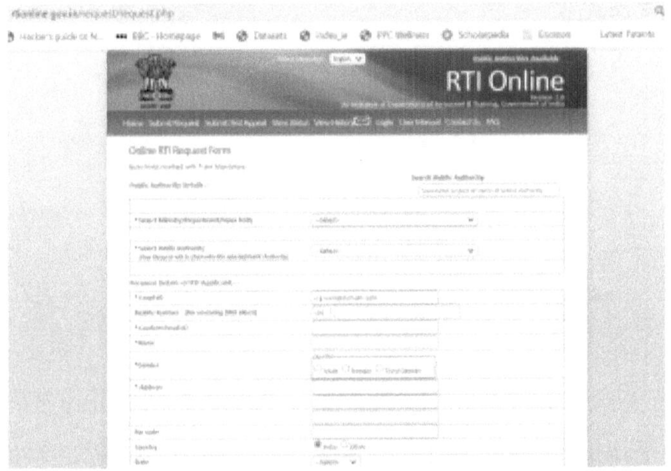

Figure: Online RTI Request form at the RTI portal

11.4 A sample RTI application

A sample RTI application is as follows:

To

The Central/Public Information Officer, RTI Office

(Address of public authority/Office)

Date:

Subject: Request to furnish information under Right to Information Act, 2005

Dear Sir/ Madam,

You are requested to furnish the following information/ documents.

1.

2.

3.

If the information is not available in your office, kindly forward to the concerned public authority as per section 6(3) of the RTI Act,2005.

I am a citizen of India and address is given below. Requisite RTI application fee for Rs.10/- paid via Indian Postal Order/ Bank Draft/ Cheque No.............. dated....................... is enclosed.

Yours sincerely,

(Name & Signature)

Address:

11.5 Conclusion

RTI laws promote government transparency and accountability, allowing citizens to access public information. In the next chapter, we will discuss filing an FIR and dealing with the police, ensuring individuals know their rights in criminal proceedings.

Chapter 12: How to File an FIR and Deal with the Police

In this chapter, we discuss your rights when dealing with the police, the steps to file an FIR, and what to do if the police refuse to help.

12.1 What is an FIR?

An FIR (First Information Report) is an official document that the police register when they receive information about a cognizable offense (a serious crime like theft, assault, or fraud). Once an FIR is registered, the police must investigate the matter.

Important: You do NOT need a lawyer to file an FIR. It is your right to file one for a crime that affects you or someone else.

12.2 Step-by-Step Guide to Filing an FIR

Step 1: Visit the Police Station

- Go to the nearest police station in the jurisdiction where the crime happened.
- Ask for the duty officer and state that you want to file an FIR.

Step 2: Give Your Statement Clearly

- Explain the incident clearly and truthfully.

- Include details like date, time, location, and description of the crime.
- If there are witnesses, mention their names and contact details.
- Provide supporting documents, photos, or CCTV footage if available.

Step 3: Ask for a Copy of the FIR

- The officer will write down your complaint.
- Read the FIR carefully before signing it to avoid incorrect details.
- Request a free copy of the FIR (as per Section 154(2) of CrPC, or Section 173 of the BNSS for matters after 1 July 2024). This is your legal right!

Pro Tip: If the police refuse to register your FIR, ask them politely to give it in writing. Most officers will avoid doing this and may register the FIR immediately.

12.3 What to do if the Police Refuse to Register the FIR?

Common Excuses Given by Police:

"This is not our jurisdiction."

Reality: Any police station must record your FIR and forward it to the correct jurisdiction.

"Come back later, the officer is busy."

Reality: They cannot delay an FIR for non-serious reasons.

"No need for an FIR, we'll handle it informally."

Reality: Always insist on an official FIR.

12.4 Your Actions If Police Refuse to File FIR

- Write a complaint to the SP (Superintendent of Police) in your district.
- File an online FIR on state police websites (most states have this option).
- Approach the nearest Magistrate's Court under Section 156(3) CrPC.
- Police Complaints Authority (PCA) exists in many states for reporting police misconduct.

12.5 Online Police Complaint: The Fastest Way to File a Complaint

Many states allow FIRs to be filed online for non-emergency cases like:

Theft/lost items (phones, wallets, etc.)

Cyber fraud (banking scams, phishing)

Harassment or stalking cases

How to File an Online FIR:

- Go to your state police website (e.g., Delhi: www.delhipolice.nic.in[1], Maharashtra: www.mahapolice.gov.in[2])

---

1. http://www.delhipolice.nic.in/

- Select 'Lodge an e-FIR' or similar option.
- Enter your details and description of the crime.
- Upload any evidence (screenshots, transaction details, etc.).
- Receive a digital acknowledgment of your FIR.

Online FIRs save time and avoid police station visits.

12.6 Your Rights When Dealing with the Police

You have the right to:

- File an FIR for free without police harassment.
- Get a copy of the FIR immediately.
- Not be forced to withdraw a complaint.
- File an FIR in any language you are comfortable with.
- Ask for the badge number and name of the officer refusing to register your complaint.

You DO NOT have to:

- Pay any bribe for registering an FIR.
- Answer unnecessary personal questions.
- Sign any blank document.

12.7 Emergency Contacts & Legal Helplines

National Police Helpline: 100

Women's Helpline: 1091

Cybercrime Helpline: 1930

---

2. http://www.mahapolice.gov.in/

Legal Aid (Free): 15100 (NALSA - Free legal service)

12.8 Quick Takeaways

- Filing an FIR is your legal right – the police cannot refuse it.
- Always ask for a free copy of your FIR.
- Online FIRs are available for certain crimes.
- If refused, escalate the complaint to higher authorities.
- Never pay a bribe or sign blank papers.
- Knowing the law = Empowering Yourself!

12.9 Conclusion

Knowing how to file an FIR ensures timely legal action and police intervention in criminal matters. Understanding police procedures can protect individuals from legal pitfalls. Next, we will discuss traffic laws and challans, helping individuals navigate road regulations and penalties.

Chapter 13: Laws Related to Traffic Rules and Challans

Traffic laws affect everyone – whether you're driving, riding a bike, or simply walking on the road. This chapter will arm you with essential knowledge about traffic challans, how to contest unfair fines, and the latest rules you need to know.

13.1 Understanding Challans & Fines

A challan is a penalty issued by the traffic police for violating traffic rules. With advancements in technology, the government now uses e-challans, which are automatically generated through cameras and traffic surveillance systems.

Types of Challans:

- Manual Challan – Issued physically by a traffic officer.
- E-Challan – Generated digitally via CCTV footage or automated traffic monitoring.

Common Traffic Fines in India

Violation	Fine Amount
Not wearing a helmet	₹1,000 & license suspension
Driving without a seatbelt	₹1,000
Using mobile while driving	₹5,000
Drunk driving	₹10,000 & possible jail
Jumping a red light	₹5,000
Overspeeding	₹1,000 - ₹2,000
No valid insurance	₹2,000

Pro Tip: If you receive an e-challan, you can verify and pay it online on your state's traffic police website. Never pay a fine in cash unless you receive an official receipt.

13.2 How to Check & Pay Your Challan Online

Did you know you might have a pending challan you weren't even aware of? With automatic cameras, many people receive challans without even being stopped. Here's how to check:

- Step 1: Visit the official government site – https://echallan.parivahan.gov.in
- Step 2: Enter your vehicle number or driving license number.
- Step 3: If any challans are pending, you will see the details and payment options.
- Step 4: Pay using UPI, net banking, or credit/debit card.

Why pay online? It prevents corruption and ensures you get an official receipt.

13.3 What If You're Wrongly Fined? How to Contest a Challan

Traffic cops are human, and mistakes happen. If you believe you received a fine unfairly, you have the right to challenge it.

Steps to Dispute a Challan:

- Gather proof – If possible, take pictures or video evidence proving your innocence.
- Visit the nearest Traffic Police Office – File a complaint and request a review.
- File an online complaint – Some states allow you to contest an e-challan via their website.
- Go to court – If the dispute is serious, you can challenge the challan in the local traffic court.

Pro Tip: If an officer insists on a fine that seems unfair, ask for their badge number and name. Corrupt officials often back down when they realize you know your rights.

13.4 Can the Police Seize Your License or Car?

Many people panic when a cop takes their license or car keys. Here's what the law says:

- A traffic cop CANNOT seize your keys or force you out of your vehicle.
- They CAN seize your license in serious violations (like drunk driving) but must provide a receipt.
- They CAN impound your vehicle in cases of No valid driving license, Drunk driving, Involvement in an

accident

Solution: If your license is taken, you can reclaim it from the RTO after paying the fine.

13.5 Your Rights When Stopped by Traffic Police

What the Police CAN Do:

- Ask for your license, insurance, and registration papers.
- Issue a challan if you violate rules.
- Conduct a breathalyser test for drunk driving.

What the Police CANNOT Do:

- Take away your car keys.
- Physically force you to pay a fine on the spot.
- Confiscate your vehicle unless you committed a serious offense.

Pro Tip: If you feel threatened, record the interaction on your phone. You have the right to do so in public places.

13.6 Emergency Contacts for Traffic Issues

- National Traffic Helpline: 103
- Delhi Traffic Police: 1095
- Mumbai Traffic Police: 100
- Bangalore Traffic Police: 103
- Legal Aid (Free): 15100 (NALSA - Free legal service)

1. **Quick Takeaways**

Never pay fines in cash without a receipt. Always check for pending e-challans online. You can dispute an unfair challan by visiting the traffic police office or filing online. Know your rights – traffic police cannot seize your keys or force payment. Recording an encounter with traffic police is legal and can protect you.

13.8 Conclusion

Traffic laws help maintain order on the roads and impose penalties for violations. Knowing your rights and obligations as a driver or pedestrian prevents legal trouble. Next, we will discuss cybercrime laws, which are crucial for staying safe in the digital world.

Chapter 14: Law Related to Cyber Crime and Online Fraud

In this chapter, we'll cover the most common cyber frauds, how to file a cyber complaint, and your legal rights under India's Information Technology (IT) Act, 2000.

14.1 Common Online Frauds & How to Avoid Them

1. Banking & UPI Frauds

Fake calls claiming to be from your bank, asking for OTPs or CVVs.

Fraudulent UPI links tricking you into sending money instead of receiving it.

What to Do: Never share OTPs, UPI PINs, or passwords. Banks never ask for them!

2. Job & Loan Scams

You get an SMS message saying "Get a job at Google! Pay ₹50,000 for training."

Instant loan offers with hidden charges that keep increasing.

What to Do: Always verify companies on LinkedIn or official websites.

3. Online Shopping & Fake Websites

You order a branded phone, but receive a brick instead.

Fake shopping sites vanish after taking payments.

What to Do: Buy only from trusted platforms like Amazon, Flipkart. Avoid unverified websites.

4. Sextortion & Blackmail

Scammers befriend you online, get personal photos, and blackmail you.

Hackers take over social media accounts and demand ransom.

What to Do: Never share personal content with strangers. Report blackmailers immediately.

5. Identity Theft & SIM Swaps

Fraudsters use stolen Aadhaar/PAN to take loans in your name.

Your SIM card suddenly stops working – someone cloned it.

What to Do: Enable SIM lock, two-factor authentication, and check your credit report regularly.

6. Digital Arrest Scam

These scams are becoming popular recently. It may start with a recorded call that your parcel is stuck at customs. Then on calling back, someone pretends to be a police official or customs official, they may even do a video call and show the insight of a fake police station or show real looking ID cards. They will say you are now under "digital arrest" and not to move out of the house and always keep the video camera on. Then they may proceed to instruct you to transfer money to them for verification of money laundering, promising it will be returned after verification. But once transferred, you never see the money again.

What to do: Never fall for the digital arrest scam. Do not transfer money. Report any such calls to the police, cybercrime cell and other authorities immediately.

14.2 How to File a Cybercrime Complaint

If you're a victim of online fraud, take immediate action. Cybercrimes are covered under the IT Act, 2000.

Step 1: Collect Evidence: Screenshots of messages, emails, transaction details, Bank statements (if money was stolen), URL of fraudulent websites or accounts.

Step 2: File a Complaint Online: Visit www.cybercrime.gov.in[1] (official Indian Cybercrime Portal). Select "Report Cyber Crime" and fill in the details. Upload supporting documents and submit.

Step 3: Report to the Police. Visit your nearest police station with a written complaint. If the police refuse to file an FIR, escalate to the Cyber Cell in your city.

Step 4: Contact Your Bank (for financial frauds). Call your bank's fraud helpline within 24 hours to block fraudulent transactions. If unauthorized money is deducted, banks are legally required to refund in most cases if reported within time.

1. https://www.cybercrime.gov.in/

14.3 Your Rights Under Cyber Laws

India's IT Act, 2000 covers various online crimes, ensuring strong legal protection.

Here are some key provisions:

- Section 66 – Hacking. Penalties include fines up to ₹5 lakh and jail.
- Section 66C – Identity theft (Penalty: 3 years jail + fine)
- Section 66D – Online fraud (Penalty: 3 years jail + ₹1 lakh fine)
- Section 67 – Publishing obscene content (Penalty: 5 years jail + ₹10 lakh fine)
- Section 72 – Data privacy violation (Penalty: 2 years jail + fine)

Use these laws to take action against scammers.

14.4 Emergency Cybercrime Helplines

Cybercrime Helpline: 1930 (24x7 Fraud Reporting). National Police Helpline: 100. Women's Cyber Safety Helpline: 1091. Bank Fraud Helpline (RBI DigiSaathi): 14431

14.5 Quick Takeaways

Never share OTPs, PINs, or passwords with anyone. Verify job offers, shopping sites, and unknown numbers before making payments. If scammed, report it immediately on cybercrime.gov.in and inform your bank. Know your rights under the IT Act, 2000 to fight online fraud. Always enable two-factor authentication for banking and social media accounts.

14.6 Digital Personal Data Protection Act, 2023 (DPDPA)

India enacted its first comprehensive data protection law – the Digital Personal Data Protection Act, 2023 (DPDPA) – on 11 August 2023. The Data Protection Board of India was established in November 2025 to enforce this law. The DPDPA is being implemented in phases, with full compliance requirements expected by 2027. This is a landmark law that every citizen interacting with digital services should know about.

The key provisions of the DPDPA that affect ordinary citizens are as follows:

Right to Know: You have the right to obtain information about how your personal data is being processed by any company or app.

Right to Correction and Erasure: You can request that incorrect personal data about you be corrected or deleted. Companies must comply within 7 days of receiving the request.

Right to Withdraw Consent: You can withdraw your consent for a company to process your personal data at any time. Once you withdraw consent, the company must stop using your data and delete it.

Right to Grievance Redressal: You can file a complaint with the Data Protection Board of India if your data rights are violated.

Obligations on Companies: Any company, app, or website that collects your personal data must obtain your consent before collecting it, use the data only for the stated purpose, protect it with adequate security measures, and delete it when it is no longer needed.

Children's Data: For anyone below the age of 18, verifiable consent from a parent or legal guardian is required before personal data can be processed.

Penalties: Non-compliance can attract penalties of up to ₹250 crore. All personal data breaches must be reported to the Data Protection Board regardless of gravity.

In practical terms, if you receive an unsolicited call or message from a company that obtained your data without your consent, or if an app shares your information with third parties without telling you, you now have a legal basis under the DPDPA to complain to the Data Protection Board of India.

14.7 Conclusion

Cyber laws protect individuals from online fraud, identity theft, and data breaches. Understanding these laws ensures safe digital interactions. In the next chapter, we will discuss consumer rights, which safeguard buyers from fraudulent sellers and defective products.

Chapter 15: Consumer Rights and E-Commerce Laws

Every day, people in India face issues like fake products, delayed deliveries, unfair billing, and misleading ads. Knowing your consumer rights can help you get refunds, replacements, and compensation without stress.

15.1 Consumer Protection Laws in India

Your rights as a consumer are protected under:

- Consumer Protection Act, 2019 – Covers refunds, defective products, unfair trade practices, and more. Note: The Consumer Protection Act, 2019 allows online complaints, eliminating the need to visit consumer courts physically.
- Legal Metrology Act, 2009 – Ensures correct weights, pricing, and labeling on goods.
- Information Technology Act, 2000 – Protects against online fraud and e-commerce scams.
- FSSAI Regulations – Ensures food safety and hygiene.

15.2 Your Basic Consumer Rights

- Right to Safety – Products you buy should not harm you (e.g., expired food, defective electronics).
- Right to Information – You must get complete

product details (e.g., MRP, ingredients, expiry date).

- Right to Choose – No company can force you into buying something you don't need.
- Right to Be Heard – You can file a complaint and demand action.
- Right to Seek Compensation – You can demand a refund, replacement, or compensation for faulty goods or poor service.
- Right to Consumer Education – Government & consumer forums must spread awareness about consumer rights.

15.3 Common Consumer Complaints & How to Handle Them

1. Online Shopping Fraud. This can include: Wrong, defective, or fake product delivered, Order cancelled by seller without refund, Item marked as "delivered" but never received,

Solution: File a complaint on the company's website or National Consumer Helpline (NCH).

2. Restaurants & Food Fraud: This includes: Service charge forcibly added to the bill, Expired or unhygienic food served, Food delivery apps like Swiggy or Zomato sending wrong/damaged food.

Solution: Lodge a complaint on www.nch.gov.in or FSSAI website for food safety issues.

3. Faulty Electronic Goods & Appliances. This can include: Fridge, AC, or mobile phone stops working soon after

purchase, Seller refuses to repair even during the warranty period, Fake brands sold as original.

Solution: Escalate through company helpline, then file a consumer complaint.

4. Telecom & Internet Issues. This includes Slow internet despite paying for high speed, Unexpected deductions from mobile balance, Unsolicited promotional calls despite DND activation.

Solution: Lodge a complaint at TRAI's portal or NCH.

5. Travel & Hotel Scams. These include Fake bookings where hotel refuses check-in, Refund denied after flight cancellation, Hidden charges added to bills.

Solution: Escalate to consumer court if the company refuses refund.

15.4 Step-by-Step Guide: How to File a Consumer Complaint

Step 1: Contact the Seller/Service Provider. Call or email customer support. Explain the issue and demand a solution. If no response within 7 days, move to the next step.

Step 2: File a Complaint on National Consumer Helpline (NCH). Call 1800-11-4000 or visit www.consumerhelpline.gov.in[1]. Select the company and explain your grievance. You'll get a complaint reference number.

---

1. https://consumerhelpline.gov.in/

Step 3: File a Case in Consumer Court (If Needed). If the company ignores your complaint, file a case in Consumer Disputes Redressal Commission. No lawyer needed for small claims. Compensation up to ₹1 crore can be claimed for damages. Note: Cases in consumer court are usually resolved within 90 days!

15.5 Where to File Your Consumer Complaint?

National Consumer Helpline (NCH): 1800-11-4000.

Consumer Court Website: www.consumerhelpline.gov.in[2]

FSSAI Food Safety Complaints: 1800-11-2100

Telecom Complaints (TRAI): 198

Online Shopping Fraud (Cyber Crime): 1930

15.6 Quick Takeaways

You have the right to demand refunds, replacements, and compensation. Always escalate complaints to the National Consumer Helpline (NCH) first. Online complaints save time—visit www.consumerhelpline.gov.in[3]. Consumer court can award compensation up to ₹1 crore for damages. Never let companies bully you into accepting bad service or fake products.

15.7 Conclusion

---

2. https://consumerhelpline.gov.in/

3. http://www.consumerhelpline.gov.in

Consumer laws protect buyers from fraud and unfair trade practices. Knowing your rights ensures you can demand fair treatment from businesses. Next, we will discuss domestic violence and protection laws, which provide legal remedies for victims of abuse.

Chapter 16: Domestic Violence & Protection Laws

Domestic violence isn't just about physical abuse—it includes verbal, emotional, financial, and mental abuse. Men, women, children, and senior citizens—everyone has legal rights to protection. This chapter will break down domestic violence laws, protection orders, and how victims can seek help.

16.1 What Counts as Domestic Violence?

Domestic violence is not just physical. The Protection of Women from Domestic Violence Act (PWDVA), 2005 defines abuse (directed against women) as follows:

- Physical Abuse – Hitting, slapping, pushing, burning, choking.
  Emotional & Verbal Abuse – Insults, threats, humiliation, name-calling.
- Sexual Abuse – Forced sex, marital rape, sexual harassment.
  Financial Abuse – Controlling money, not allowing the victim to work.
- Neglect & Abandonment – Denying basic needs, throwing someone out of the house.

16.2 Legal Protections Under Domestic Violence Laws

In India, victims are protected under:

- Protection of Women from Domestic Violence Act (PWDVA), 2005 – Provides protection orders, monetary compensation, and housing rights to women.
- Section 498A of IPC (Section 85 of BNS for matters after 1 July 2024) – Criminalizes cruelty against married women.
- The Maintenance & Welfare of Parents and Senior Citizens Act, 2007 – Protects senior citizens from abuse.
- Juvenile Justice Act – Protects children from domestic violence.

16.3 What Can a Victim Do? How to Get Protection

Step 1: In case of domestic violence against women, contact a Protection Officer or Women's Helpline. Call 181 (Women's Helpline) or 1091 (Domestic Violence Helpline). Protection Officers will help victims get emergency support and legal aid.

Step 2: File a Domestic Violence Complaint. Go to the nearest police station or Women's Cell. Mention details of the abuse—date, time, incidents, and witnesses. Police will register a case under PWDVA, 2005 or Section 498A of IPC (Section 85 of BNS for matters after 1 July 2024).

Step 3: Apply for a Protection Order. Protection Orders stop the abuser from contacting or harming the victim. Victims can file an application in the Magistrate's Court with the help of a lawyer or NGO. Courts can order abusers to stay away from the victim's home, workplace, and children.

16.4 Rights of Senior Citizens Against Family Abuse

Elderly parents often face harassment from their own children.

- Under The Maintenance & Welfare of Parents and Senior Citizens Act, 2007: Parents (aged 60+) can demand monthly maintenance from their children.
- They can apply for protection if facing mental or financial abuse.
- Children can be legally evicted from the house if they harass their parents.
- If elderly parents are being mistreated, they can file a case in the Maintenance Tribunal.

16.5 What If the Victim is a Non Senior Citizen Man? Do Men Have Protection?

While most domestic violence laws protect women, and senior citizens have their own protection, men can also file complaints for abuse under:

- Section 323 IPC (Section 115 of BNS) – If physically assaulted.
- Section 506 IPC (Section 351 of BNS) – If threatened or mentally harassed.
- Section 125 CrPC (Section 144 of BNSS) – If denied financial support from spouse.

16.6 What If the Victim is a Child? Protection for Minors

Children facing domestic violence can seek protection under:

- Juvenile Justice Act – Protects minors from abuse, neglect, and exploitation.
- POCSO Act – Punishes sexual abuse against minors.
- National Child Helpline (1098) – Offers free, emergency rescue services for abused children.

Note: If a child is being mistreated, anyone, not just the victim, can report it to 1098 for immediate action.

16.7 Emergency Helplines for Domestic Violence Victims

National Women's Helpline: 181

Domestic Violence Helpline: 1091

Senior Citizen Helpline: 14567

Child Helpline: 1098

Police Emergency Helpline: 100

Legal Aid (Free): 15100 (NALSA)

16.8 Quick Takeaways

- Domestic violence includes physical, mental, emotional, and financial abuse.
- Victims can get Protection Orders, residence rights, and financial compensation.
- Senior citizens can demand financial support and protection from abusive children.
- Men and children can also seek legal protection against domestic abuse.
- You don't need to leave your home—courts can order

the abuser to leave instead.

16.9 Conclusion

Domestic violence laws safeguard victims from abuse and provide legal recourse for protection and justice. Knowing these rights is crucial for personal safety. In the next chapter, we will explore the steps involved in a civil court case in India.

Chapter 17: Steps in a Civil Court Case in India

In this chapter, we briefly go through the steps in a civil court case. The procedure in different Indian courts for civil cases is broadly the same.

This is for normal cases. Note that Public Interest Litigations or PILs allow any citizen to file cases for public welfare in the Supreme Court or High Court.

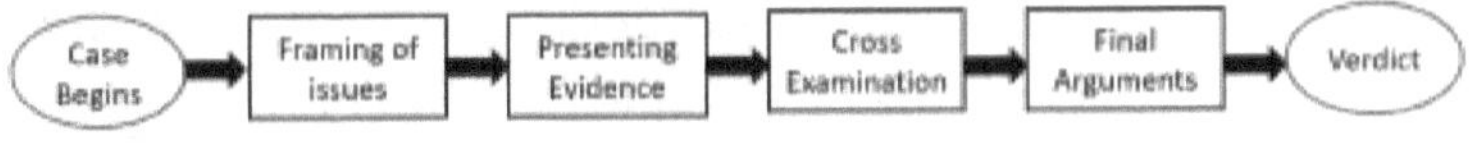

Figure: Different stages of a civil court case in India

17.1 Filing of the civil case

The first step is to file the civil case in any of the courts such as district court or high court etc. One should ideally employ a good lawyer to file the court case in the proper format and using the correct legal terminology. The petitioner is the person(s) who have filed the case and the respondent(s) or defendant is the person against whom the case is filed.

17.2 Summons to the parties

Upon filing of the civil case, the court gives summons to the respondent parties and other interested parties to appear in the court on the next date of the hearing, failing which the case shall be decided ex-parte.

17.3 First hearing

On the first hearing date, both the parties, the petitioners and the respondents, with their lawyers, appear in the court. The respondents are given time to file their responses to the petition.

17.4 Framing of the issues

Once both the petitioner and respondent have filed their respective statements with the court, the judge begins by identifying and framing the issues of disagreement between the two parties. These are the issues on which the court will give its verdict.

17.5 Presenting evidence

The next step is the evidence presentation. Both the parties file their evidence in various formats to support their case. Usually it is written evidence, however oral evidence and electronic evidence such as video recordings and audio recordings, photos etc. may also be filed.

17.6 Cross examination

The cross examination is part of the presenting evidence stage. When a party brings a witness to give their oral evidence, the lawyer of the opposite party cross examines the witness on various points. A skillful lawyer can frame their questions in such a way as to discredit the evidence of the opposite party witness.

17.7 Final arguments

At the end of the evidence presentation and the cross examination of the witnesses of both the parties: petitioners and respondents, the parties get a chance to file their final arguments in the court. These arguments can take into account the opposite party's arguments and witness testimonies.

17.8 Pronunciation of verdict

At the end of the process, the judge takes into account all the evidence and oral witness testimonies, all the arguments presented, the law that is applicable and finally pronounces their verdict.

17.9 Appeals

In case one of the parties is not happy with the verdict, they have the option of appealing the verdict in a higher court, such as a high court or supreme court. The process continues until the parties have exhausted their appeals process.

17.10 Conclusion

In this chapter, we have gone through the various steps of a court case. Often, the cases take many years to complete all these steps and reach a verdict and after the appeals process has been exhausted. Understanding civil court procedures helps individuals navigate legal disputes efficiently. Knowing how to file a case and present evidence ensures justice is served. Next, we will explore websites and apps that provide legal advice, making legal help more accessible.

Chapter 18: Websites and Apps to get Legal Advice

In this chapter we discuss a few available resources where a person can access to get legal information and advice.

18.1 Free or Low-cost legal advice websites

There are a number of websites available for getting free or low-cost legal advice from lawyers in India. Such websites can be used by people as needed. However, the quality of such advice varies. One can leverage the viewpoints of multiple lawyers to get a general idea of what to do and to make sure one is not going in the wrong direction.

The procedure to log a legal query is as follows: one has to visit the website, create a free account by filling some basic details. After that, one can log one's query, which will be answered by the lawyers within a few hours. Some of the advocates may send private messages or directly call the person logging the complaint, rather than reply on the public forum. Also, they may ask for a fee for their advice, or pressurize the person to hire them as a lawyer.

Examples of free legal advice websites include the following:

• Lawrato: https://lawrato.com/free-legal-advice

• Indian Kanoon https://www.kaanoon.com/

- Vkeel https://www.vkeel.com/

- Vidhikarya https://www.vidhikarya.com/

Of these, Lawrato seems to have many lawyers relying to each query promptly and in the public.

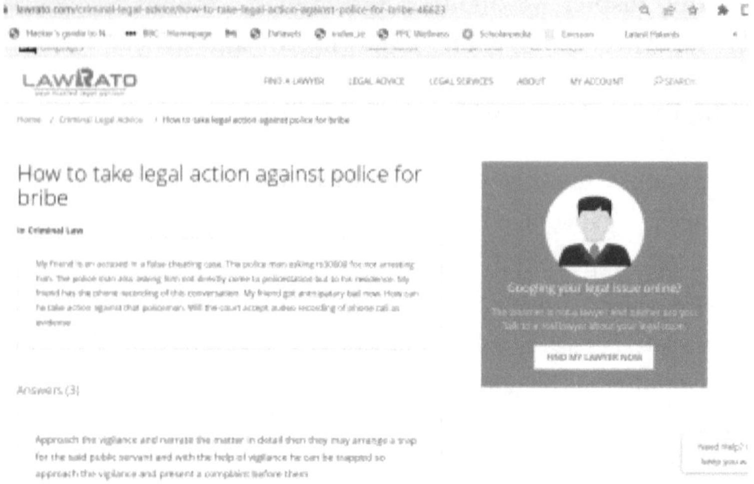

Figure: Screenshot for the lawrato website for getting legal advice for queries

Figure: Screenshot for the Indiankanoon website for getting relevant judgments in Indian courts for various topics

Indian Kanoon is a very good resource for accessing past court judgements on various topics.

18.2 Legal apps

There are a few good apps in the Google play store and Apple App store where a person can learn about relevant laws, improve their knowledge on law and get help related to their case.

One can download and install these apps in one's phone to get good legal information and learn about the laws in India.

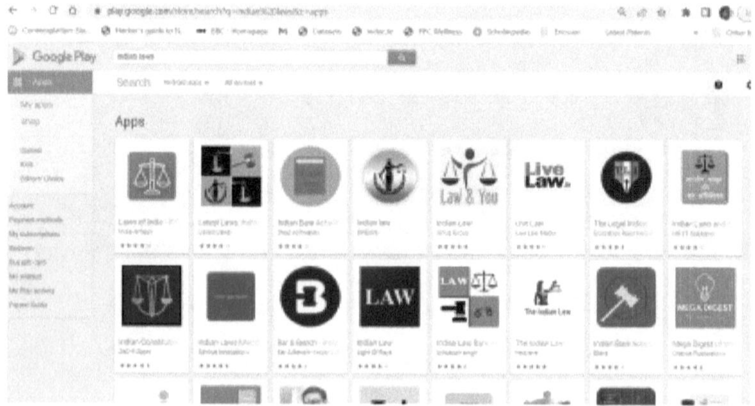

Figure: Apps related to Indian laws in the Google play store

Some such apps include the following:

- Indian Bare Acts (Indian Law)
- Laws of India - IPC, CPC, CrPC, MVA, IEA & Acts
- Indian Constitution Law's, Indian law and acts
- Bar & Bench - Indian Legal News
- Live Law

One can go to the google play store and search for such apps using keywords such as "Indian laws" or specific topics such as "Property law India" or "criminal law India".

18.3 Conclusion

Legal websites and apps make legal guidance accessible to everyone. Knowing where to seek legal advice can save time and effort. In the next chapter, we will discuss how to handle lawyers effectively to ensure the best legal representation.

Chapter 19: How to Handle Lawyers

Often when we are dealing with matters of law, it is important to get a qualified lawyer to fight our case. In this chapter we discuss some issues related to lawyers.

19.1 Getting a Lawyer vs Party in Person

One choice we have to make is whether to get a lawyer to fight our case or do it ourselves.

There are many advantages to hiring a lawyer. The lawyer knows about the procedures in the courts and might be experienced in the area where our court case is pending, such as property law or family law or criminal law. Lawyers can be helpful to us in various matters related to our court case such as bail, filing petitions, filing replies, cross examination and so on.

Finding a suitable and good lawyer can sometimes be difficult. If our lawyer turns out to be less than ideal and takes huge fees without helping us much in the court case, that can be a problem. A bad lawyer may not deal with our case with sufficient seriousness and timeliness, or not argue our case well before the judge.

Other problems with lawyers include the following:

• Our lawyer might be not experienced in the specific area of law that the court case deals with.

- They might be too much busy with multiple cases from multiple clients to fight our case properly.

- They may lose interest in the case as time drags on.

- They might treat us (the client) as a cash cow and encourage us to file more cases that do not bring any concrete results but just increase the time and costs and cause additional stress.

- They might not be familiar with new technology and how to e-file a case or use emails or attend virtual hearings.

- They might be overconfident and overbearing and not listen to the client's needs, insisting that they know what is best, and thus harm the client's position.

- They might simply refuse to act as per the instructions from the client, selecting the course of action that require least effort for themselves.

- Worst of all, they may sometimes even collude with the opposite party and compromise the case at crucial points.

The other option is to not get a lawyer at all and fight our own case as a Party in Person (PIP). The advantage of fighting our own case as a party in person is that we can make our own choices and argue our own case before the judge and not have to worry about issues related to lawyers such as high lawyer fees or our lawyer being inexperienced or not able to represent our case properly. However, with PIP we have the disadvantage of not being familiar with the procedures and the forms and steps needed for our petition and have to learn everything from scratch as it goes. It can be a steep learning curve to fight our own case as party in person.

19.2 Choosing a good lawyer for fighting our court cases

One important strategy for court cases is to get a good and competent lawyer whom we can trust to fight our cases.

We should engage a lawyer who is competent and has prior experience in dealing with such cases in his or her career. We should make sure our lawyer keeps themselves abreast of current knowledge in law including recent judgments, is comfortable with technology such as email and remote hearings. Considering that remote hearings and e-filings have become more common nowadays with the Covid-19 pandemic and are here to stay even after the pandemic is over, we should make sure that our lawyer too should be comfortable with this.

The most important quality in our chosen lawyer is that they should listen to us and be ready to act as per our instructions. They should not have the attitude that they always know what is best, but rather they should be humble, open minded and respect the fact that the client knows best about his or her own case.

19.3 Managing our lawyer

We should try to skillfully manage the lawyer during the conduct of the case, including negotiating the fees in advance, giving proper incentives and so on. We should also try to be friendly with our lawyer and not pick up fights with them over petty issues. If we decide to change the lawyer, we should try to do so amicably and without fighting.

We can also use our lawyer in additional skillful ways, such as sending them to attend the court dates instead of us and avoid unnecessary travel and expenses of our own.

19.4 Changing our lawyer

We should also not be attached to any one lawyer and be ready to change our lawyer if the need arises, for example if we realize that the current lawyer is no longer able to effectively represent our case.

As per the Indian laws, the existing lawyer cannot stop us from changing our lawyer, even if they do not provide a "No Objection Certificate". We can always file a new Wakalatnama in the court whenever we need, certifying that the new lawyer will represent us in this case instead of the old lawyer. We should always keep this in mind.

Having said that, it is also not a good practice to change lawyers too frequently during the case. Having chosen a lawyer, we should not have undue expectations on them and give them some time to prove themselves. We should also try to be amicable with the old lawyer while changing the lawyer.

19.5 Conclusion

In this chapter, we have looked at some of the important aspects of handling a lawyer for our court case, including how to select a good lawyer and how to manage and change them if needed. If we keep all these aspects in mind, then handling the lawyer can be manageable for us. Finally, in the next chapter we conclude this book by summarizing key learnings and encouraging legal awareness in everyday life.

Chapter 20: Conclusion

In this book, we have discussed a few specific cases from daily life in which the laws are applicable, such as in relation to marriage, employment, credit cards, inheritance, discrimination, contracts and inheritance. We have also looked at some practical aspects such as handling a lawyer and using apps and websites to get legal knowledge.

It is important for all citizens to become familiar with how the laws affect them. This is the only solution to demand their rights under the law and under the Indian constitution.

One can also take the help of search engines like google and legal websites such as indiankanoon.com (which has judgments by high courts and supreme courts concerning different topics) and apps and websites such as lawrato.com (where one can ask lawyers for advice) for the purpose. Use of RTIs is another good tool for citizens to get the relevant information from the government departments.

Legal awareness is an essential tool for every citizen. Understanding everyday laws—from contracts to consumer rights—empowers individuals to navigate legal situations with confidence. By staying informed, one can safeguard their rights, seek justice when needed, and contribute to a more legally aware society.

About the Author

Siva Prasad Bose is an author of various introductory guidebooks related to aspects of Indian laws. He is currently retired after many years of service in Uttar Pradesh Power Corporation Limited. He received his engineering degree from Jadavpur University, Kolkata and has a law degree from Meerut University, Meerut. His interests lie in the fields of family law, civil law, law of contracts, and areas of law related to electricity generation and revenue related issues.

Other Books by Siva Prasad Bose

Introduction to Wills and Probate

Senior Citizens Abuse in India

Introduction to Negotiable Instruments

Introduction to Marriage Laws in India

Neighbor Problems in India and what to do about them

Managing Court Cases with Mental Strength

Delays in Court Cases in India

Self-Publish Books and E-Books in India

Introduction to Patents and Patent Law in India

Introduction to Property Law in India

Don't miss out!

Visit the website below and you can sign up to receive emails whenever Siva Prasad Bose publishes a new book. There's no charge and no obligation.

https://books2read.com/r/B-A-RVCN-REQWB

BOOKS2READ

Connecting independent readers to independent writers.

Did you love *Introduction to Street Law in India*? Then you should read *Property Disputes in Indian Families*[1] by Siva Prasad Bose and Joy Bose!

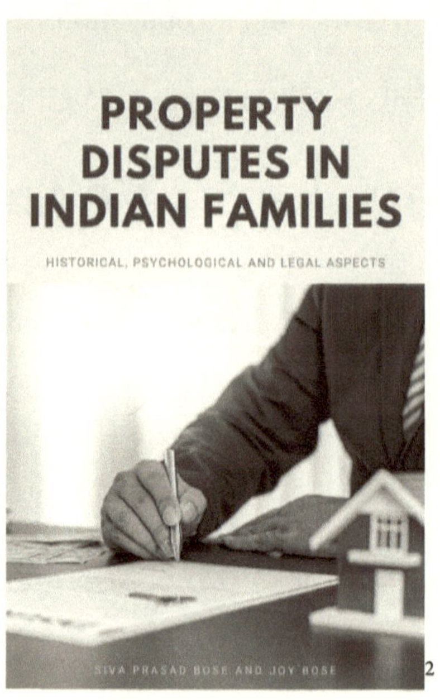

[2]

Property disputes are one of the most common, and most emotionally devastating, legal conflicts in Indian families.

Whether siblings are fighting over ancestral land, relatives are contesting a will, or Non-Resident Indians are struggling to protect assets from thousands of miles away, these disputes consume years, drain finances, and permanently fracture relationships.

---

1. https://books2read.com/u/bMY5Lv

2. https://books2read.com/u/bMY5Lv

In this insightful and practical guide, the authors explore the historical, psychological, and legal dimensions of property disputes in Indian families, drawing on real case studies, landmark court judgments, and decades of legal experience.

What this book covers:

The History of Property Disputes — From the epic rivalries of the Ramayana and Mahabharata to the high-profile feuds of the Ambani, Birla, and Singhania families, property battles have shaped Indian history at every level of society.

The Psychology Behind Family Conflicts — How childhood dynamics, parental favouritism, sibling rivalry, and deep-seated feelings of entitlement set the stage for bitter legal battles decades later.

Understanding Property Laws in India — A clear, accessible guide to the Indian Succession Act 1925, the Transfer of Property Act 1882, intestate succession, wills, probate, and more.

Fighting Property Cases in Court — Step-by-step guidance on navigating litigation: choosing the right lawyer, managing finances, handling cross-examination, and avoiding deliberate delay tactics.

Women's Rights in Property — The legal reforms, landmark Supreme Court rulings, and persistent real-world challenges that define women's inheritance rights in modern India.

NRI Property Issues — How overseas Indians can safeguard their assets against encroachment, Power of Attorney abuse, fraudulent transfers, and the ever-present threat of adverse possession.

Alternative Dispute Resolution (ADR) — Why mediation, arbitration, and Lok Adalats are often faster, cheaper, and kinder to family relationships than years of court litigation.

Whether you are an individual navigating a family inheritance dispute, a lawyer advising clients on property matters, or an NRI trying to protect assets back home, this book gives you the knowledge, legal clarity, and practical tools to safeguard your rights, and, where possible, preserve the relationships that matter most.

About the Author

Siva Prasad Bose is an electrical engineer by profession. He is currently retired after many years of service in Uttar Pradesh Power Corporation Limited. He received his engineering degree from Jadavpur University, Kolkata and has a law degree from Meerut University, Meerut. His interests lie in the fields of family law, civil law, law of contracts, and any areas of law related to power electricity related issues.

Read more at https://sivaprasadbose.wordpress.com/.